MY LITTLE BOOK OF GRIEF

By Tracey Dene Powell

My Little Book of Grief

Written by Tracey Dene Powell
Illustrations by Kevin Becken
Cover design by Kevin Becken

ISBN: 979-8-9866371-2-9

Published by BC Books, LLC
Franklin, Wisconsin, USA
Brenda E. Cortez, Publisher
Jean Sime, Publishing Coordinator

bcbooksllc.com

Quantity orders can be emailed to: brenda@bcbooksllc.com

Contents

Testimonials   6

Message from Illustrator Kevin Becken   8

Dedication   9

Foreword by Dr Gillian Ennis   11

Introduction   13

POEMS

AND SO IT IS   14

POEM FOR BOB'S 'ORDER OF SERVICE'   17

WEIRD THINGS HAPPEN   18

I AM DISCOVERING…   21

I FEEL LIKE I AM WALKING…   21

SAYING GOODBYE   23

TEARS   25

SNOWDROPS   27

THE MIRROR   29

THE CROSS   31

YET AGAIN I CRUMBLE   33

THE COLOURS OF GRIEF   35

PLEASE, WHAT DO YOU WANT?   37

WHEN YOU ARE IN THE GRIP OF SORROW   39

COME BACK   41

LETTING GO   43

THE SKYLARK   45

THE GRAVE   47

BLACKBIRD   49

POEMS (con't)

CONFUSION	51
THE CIRCLE	53
I TALK WITH YOU A LOT	55
THE STALKER	63
SWEET DREAMS	65
YOUR HOUSE	67
SOMETIMES	69
CAN'T BEAR THE THOUGHT	71
THE FLOWER	73
CONSTANTLY DANCING	75
THERE WILL BE TIMES IN LIFE	77
FRIENDS	79
THE LAST TIME	81
LIFE GOES ON	83
THE CLIFF FACE	85
THE BUTTERFLY	87
BORROW YOUR RAINBOW	89
THIS LIFE IS NOT THE END	91
A PIECE OF MY HEART	93
Acknowledgements and Thanks	95
About the Author	97

Testimonials

Tracey's poetry is absolutely beautiful and so sincere. What makes this so gorgeous and real is the fact you can clearly feel in the words, that it comes from one who has suffered and clearly continues to suffer. This level of authenticity is not often seen in many grief poems and readings out there, so this is grief in its absolute ugliest yet purest form.

It's a beautiful masterpiece of a personal journey that doesn't hold back; it's so wrapped up in itself it makes you want to keep reading; read on for reassurance that things are in some way going to improve despite the brutal honesty that is present throughout.

Shane Mousley, Funeral Director, Butterfly Funerals

In order to appreciate the good times and joyous things in life, we unfortunately have to have tragedies and heartbreak. Tracey's honesty is what makes her book so real and thought provoking. The message it portrays can help all of us to put our lives into perspective and come to terms with bereavement and loss.

Matt Hampson OBE, Matt Hampson Foundation

These poems are extremely moving and really quite hard to read at times - such is the raw emotion coming off the page. Never more so than in "The Mirror" and "Yet Again I Crumble". But every poem - even the bleakest - offers a catharsis simply by so honestly expressing such devastation: merely bringing the pain into the light weakens its power. I'm sure that others who are grieving, when they read your words, will find relief in recognising they are NOT alone in experiencing such despair. But more than that, they will flourish in seeing there IS hope and though the pain never entirely passes, one does move on. As you testify, I think this is what I like best in the poems - the fact that the hope which is undeniably there (in "Come Back" and "The Grave" especially) is not a simple switch which turns off everything else, but a gradual moving on; to higher ground, out of the dark woods, and to a place where new possibilities lie.

William Ivory, leading film, television and theatre writer

Through the honesty of her poignant and powerful poetry, Tracey has allowed the reader into parts of her journey through an acute year of grief. In these stark glimpses, we see the rawness of new grief stirring up the painful debris of past bereavements with that of the current storm, we see the everchanging landscape of grief, and recognise the need to learn to take each step slowly and with care.

I pray that Tracey's courage in sharing her journey will encourage others when feeling lost, frightened, and in despair at the sheer weight and darkness of grief. The journey of grief is a part of life; may we know that we do not travel alone and that "light shines in the darkness and the darkness does not overcome it" (John's gospel chapter 1 verse 5).

Bless you and thank you Tracey.

Reverend Deborah Marsh, Vicar of Whissendine

Tracey's book is her personal journey, but others reading it will find hope and relate with their feelings of grief, which will help them know they are not alone.

Gill McNab, Dallas, Texas

I followed Tracey's cathartic journey in verse from the rawness of early grief, anger, and pain to calm reflection and acknowledgement that love and memory endure. An excellent read for anyone in the wilderness of bereavement. After darkness and despair, the sun will shine again.

Jackie Lymn Rose, Funeral Director, A W Lymn

My word, Tracey is so lovely and talented, and that has made reading all of her poems all the more special. The world is a better place for people like Tracey, and I sincerely hope these poems help someone else who is finding their way with grief.

Tom Johnson - Funeral Director, E M Dormans

Tracey invited me to illustrate her poetry. Her accounts of grief were so personal, and so intense, I feel privileged to have been granted an open window into her mind. Such a sombre subject was not something I have illustrated before. The feelings are raw, honest, confusing, enlightening, and a challenge to represent. I opened my mind, read the text, and images appeared with freedom. I captured what I felt - devastation, dark sadness, rough and shaky discomfort, and reassuringly, hope.

Kevin Becken

www.kbart.co.uk
kevin.becken@kbart.co.uk

Dedicated to Bob Sheridan.

When Covid hit in 2020 I spent many afternoons with Bob as part of his caring bubble, which fermented into a deep and profound friendship. We enjoyed writing and music together, and we became special confidantes. He became not only the dearest friend I could wish for, but also my mentor and father figure. I will be forever grateful for what we had.

Foreword

By Dr Gillian Ennis (retired General Practitioner)

Any bereaved reader will immediately connect with the emotions documented throughout Tracey's poems. A terrifying and real glimpse into the true pain of loss. I found myself glancing at, re-reading, and fully immersing myself in the poems again and again.

Tracey's honest and perceptive descriptions of the oscillating moods experienced in grief allow the reader to recognise, explore, and make more sense of their own situation.

Above all, this journey in poetry offers hope and encouragement as we see glimmers of healing emerge.

I will be gifting 'My Little Book of Grief' many times in the future. Thank you, Tracey

Introduction

On the 14th December 2020, my heart stopped; I began a journey of raw grief. Losing someone you love destroys your life, everything becomes meaningless… a struggle. This book is the private collection of my personal poetry, written whilst going through heartbreak and desperation. At my lowest, the pain was so suffocating that I didn't want to go on. But I survived. And so will you.

I am using my poems to reach out… to offer help through my words. My message is simple, "Never give up… let the tears flow, be gentle with yourself, you will survive this."

With love and Angel Blessings,

Tracey Dene Powell

5th November 2021

AND SO IT IS

I'm still walking this hard terrain, this never-ending road to peace
But I do feel different now; somehow more together with my senses
No matter how inconsistent my feelings can be, I seem more settled
More able to rationalise, more capable to see what acceptance is

It hasn't been easy, this road, this path, this existence I have entered
Taking tentative steps forward, weary ones back; going around in circles
Often losing my direction, my compass on life, feeling completely lost
Utterly exhausted physically; mentally fighting emotional reprisals

Although trying to be sure footed, I've often tripped and fallen hard
Spent days just nursing my wounds, assessing the best route to take
Before getting back up again, looking around and venturing forward
In the hope that I reach a bit further before I fall again and break

I remember the many times when reaching yet another cliff face of grief
Body and mind depleted from the sheer desperation of just hanging on
I would surprisingly gain the strength of Goliath and climb that vital height
To reach the summit; no victory found; for this road goes on and on and on

I've learned that some mountains of sorrow are just too high to attempt
To climb over; or conquer; or rise to the challenge and try and overcome
I've learned that sometimes the best thing is to just rest, lean against it for a while
And find another pathway; another passage around to eventually see the sun

The pathways are steep, narrow, uneven; one stumble causes such piercing pain

But I've continued to walk on; limping; crawling for what seems an unforgiving time

And now? Well now I am standing, gazing back on grief's bleak and lifeless landscape

To discover a personal inner acceptance; unreliably real; but very definitely mine

An acceptance that I have survived thus far, despite the falls and bruises I've incurred

An acceptance to hear your voice again, just the way you want; willing me to keep the fight

An acceptance where you want me to be happy again but I do need to want that too

An acceptance to accept that grief is part of me now, but I mustn't let it own me outright

8th January 2021 – Poem for Bob's 'Order of Service'

Death is nothing but a doorway; that opens when our time is right
Allowing our souls to enter through and be filled with love and light
For it is true, our journey is never ending and as mystical as the skies
We can leave behind our memories but need to cut the ties

So please do not cling onto a body that is now in an empty form
For I am not there; I am with Angels and my soul has been reborn
But instead behold all the wonders of nature; enjoy what the seasons bring
For it is there that you will find me; yes, I am all around in everything

Never forget I am always with you and let my love shine in your smile
And though tears will fall and your sorrow is raw, it will lessen after a while
Just remember how much I loved you and I know that you loved me
And we will meet again when the time is right and your own doorway you will see

8th February 2021

WEIRD THINGS HAPPEN

Weird things happen with grief, a miscellaneous sequence of coincidences
Only some may see these differently and state them clearly as significances

A song played twice, a connected song, is there a meaningful message here?
Or a watch that suddenly works, a robin by your side, a sign that you are near?

Perhaps the mind plays tricks, am I just reaching out for something to believe?
A desperate need to feel you with me, to reach out to something I can't conceive?

Your photograph which sits beside my bed, beckons me to talk each lonely night
And so I beg you to return to me, help me, comfort me, make everything alright

I chastise you, plead with you, wish I'd never met you, spitefully call your bluff
Challenging any kind of oddness to occur so I can hear you say "enough is enough"

But there is only silence and your smile taken at that moment teases me as if to say
I understand my darling, I'm hurting too and I promise we will be together again some day

My mood is as ever changing as the weather, some days heavy, some days bright

Often hours never able to feel the sun, but then the odd cloud dares to let in the light

But constant is the weight, the heaviness, the lump inside that creeps upon my breast to rest

To crush my lungs, my heart, my soul, to leave me weakened, weary and utterly bereft

Will a pain such as this ever rescind, will I ever be strong enough to beat this woeful state?

Will I ever dance happy again, step bravely, joyfully to the tune that continues to play out my fate?

Or feel the promise of a tomorrow that heals, a future that excites and restores the passion in me?

I think I read in your eyes the answer I seek; "I am always here, be the person I love, live your life, be happy, be free"

8th February 2021

I AM DISCOVERING...

I am discovering that grief is when you want to die and yet fight to stay alive, both at the same time.

It's when you can see the road ahead, but remain blind to which direction to take.

It's that sea of cold sorrow that penetrates deep enough to freeze the heart and yet burns into the soul.

It's the place where all you can do is ask God and the Angels to watch over you, and help ease the pain caused from losing and loving so much.

8th February 2021

I FEEL LIKE I AM WALKING...

I feel like I am walking on a narrow path along the edge of a mountain ridge. If I tread carefully and take my time, I should be ok. I try to keep focused on the beautiful scenery ahead of me, keeping faith that I will eventually reach the end of my journey and will be able to see everything in its full glory again. It's when I look down over the ridge that the problems begin, for that's when I feel unbalanced and drawn to stepping off the path altogether. It's not easy this path of grief and my mountain is a tough climb but I am finding that I am praying more and discovering a new relationship with God... which is interesting.

9th February 2021

SAYING GOODBYE (written for my dear friend)

There are 86,400 seconds in a day, and 1000 milliseconds in a second
And nobody can ever predict when time will eventually stop;
You cannot guard against it, prepare for that heart stopping moment
Or accept, believe or willingly forgive when your whole life will be cropped

Tomorrow is a lifetime away, unthinkable for those left behind
With sobbing and fighting the pain the only means to cope
And the lesson, if any, becomes an enemy hard to understand
Especially when the ground disappears with heaven the only hope

The favourite chair, those loving looks, remain forever a reminder
Of something that was living, real, sacred beyond any belief;
And though these memories are handed to the years to heal
That final second when time stood still will offer no remedy of relief

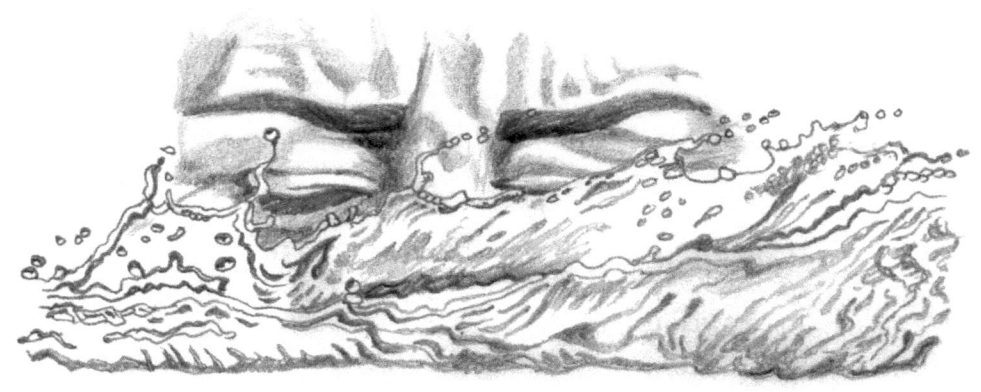

16th February 2021

TEARS

Some say that tears are only grief with nowhere else to go
And some say they are but a safety valve for the heart
But my tears come from a raging storm of pain
That has never abated from the moment we were apart

From way down in the depth of my being this storm is striking
With a sea of tears crashing against the walls of my chest
The waves of grief relentless in their force to destroy
Everything that I ever held within me as best

And it is in those moments of despair and exhaustion
That those saving tears with nowhere else to go
Will weaken the barriers that hold back this torrent storm
To allow the raging ocean of tears within me flow

22nd February 2021

SNOWDROPS

White as snow, as resilient as Spring, have you been sent from heaven sweet seed?
For you appear like a ghost in the hedgerow, to shine in our hour of need

How dark have been the nights, how void of life have been the days
Winter sets out to test our inner strength in so many dreadful ways

And then, like a prayer, you show promise of new life, a brighter day ahead
For though immersed in a frozen dark existence you chose the light instead

A lesson perhaps to teach us faith; the will to survive, or just a belief in heavenly love
To always hold onto hope when it's cold and dark; to trust in our loving Father above

Your flowers appear like magic, often in hidden lost places; I strangely wonder why?
Why you have chosen sometimes a remote and lonely place to let your beauty lie?

The seeds planted, from wherever they came, surely arrived nurtured with love and care
That I am left to believe your presence is holy; and I am here witnessing God's very own seeds of prayer

26th February 2021

THE MIRROR

I saw a person I hardly recognised today, staring back at me in the mirror of dread

A face so drawn and lifeless, so old and desperate as it reflects again, he's dead, he's dead

I seem to have aged so much; worn away so rapidly, my youth evaporating away as the tears

Continue to erode the cliffs of my cheeks and I watch helpless as the light in my eyes disappears

I wonder if I will ever repair or has grief claimed yet another victory against my will to survive

How I long for the past to sweep me up and throw me back, back to the time I felt alive

Alone we sit, just the mirror and me, with yet another confrontation, a battle of wills to fight

Should I still try to talk to the face, offer it help or once again turn my back on its hopeless plight

But I gaze, I talk, I listen to my inner voice and beg for whatever strength left to come along

For beauty is surely not in skin or an ageless search, but in a broken heart that is fighting to be strong

1st March 2021

THE CROSS

In times of worry, in hopeless despair, when the weight of pain drags you weary

And every goodness is squeezed; crushed out of your heart so you're unable to see anything clearly

When you feel alone without any hope and dark days trap your heart in the shadow

Let the wonder of spiritual love shine through to heal, to comfort; surround your head like a halo

Yes, let The Cross tell its story, listen well to the message for it will surely serve you well

And strengthen you on life's journey; allay your curiosity of the universe, heaven and hell

For Christians, it represents a devoted love, a sacrifice so we may flourish in God's eyes

A reminder that all suffering and pain is understood, especially at times when a loved one dies

But for some, The Cross gives yet another message; of destiny and a reminder of the choices made

Decisions and consequences that have mapped out our paths; support for the times we have prayed

For The Cross represents the compass of the world; a visual concept of north, south, east and west

And whenever we reach another crossroad in life, then God's message can be heard at its best

Like an arrow, follow The Cross, move forward in love and light, never forgetting the gift that is given

The wonder of nature seen every day and the faith that loved ones lost are safely held in heaven

2nd March 2021

YET AGAIN I CRUMBLE

Yet again I crumble, I break, I cry out "Come back, please come back", for yet again I feel totally lost

Caught in the net of grief that strings me up; I am dangling, helpless, soulless, counting the cost

Of losing you, saying goodbye or should I say letting go, setting free, it's just a mere medley of words

That tumble out, evaporate, dissolve with every breath that escapes from my heart's constant swirls

Not knowing what is left to heal, or what is right to hold onto, which direction I should take; it's cruel

To have such a constant confusion, a lack of trust, a relentless longing; yes, grief is making me a fool

But a fool is better than being destroyed, more respectable than giving up, or a subject of pity to see

So, "Come back, please come back," save me, reach out by any means and help this sad fool let it be

4th March 2021

THE COLOURS OF GRIEF

I once was welcoming and uplifting as a daffodil, my yellow solar plexus shining bright

I knew who I was and what I could be and everything in my world was right

But then you were gone and a fog of grief swallowed me whole, reducing all that I am

And the colour of blue surrounded me, leaving me stranded, alone and utterly damned

How could I function with my chakras so badly bruised? I couldn't, I tried but sadly failed

For my heart was broken and swallowed up with so much pain, my life source felt old and stale

But mother nature brings a healing hand as my colours of blue and yellow become slowly fused

And so now I find that green is now my saviour colour and my heart chakra is calling out for a truce

And although the fight of the colours will still go on and my recovery will be long and painfully slow

I pray that my heart chakra will travel through the blue and my daffodil yellow will once again glow

12th March 2021

PLEASE, WHAT DO YOU WANT?

Lord, bless those who have fallen, who are broken, who cry out to thee

"Lord PLEASE have mercy, what do you want from me?"

Lord, protect the weak, those who are fragile in body and mind who cry out to thee

"Lord please have mercy, WHAT do you want from me?"

Lord, reach out to those who are lost, seek out those in deep need who cry out to thee

"Lord please have mercy, what DO you want from me?"

Lord, forgive those who falter, the confused, those lacking in love who never cry out to thee

"Lord please have mercy, what do YOU want from me?"

Lord, guide me, now and forever, lead the way so I may always cry out to thee

"Lord God of mercy, in my limited life, I will try to be everything you WANT of me"

12th March 2021

WHEN YOU ARE IN THE GRIP OF SORROW

"When you are in the grip of sorrow, just remember that the arms of an Angel will always be trying to loosen it"

The coat that
once smothered
me no longer fits

19th March 2021

COME BACK

I've collected elements of grief, stored them up, stacked them together so they rested heavy in my heart

Allowed their weight to suffocate, crush, block any vein of strength that tried to save me from falling apart

I have stared up at starless skies, lost in thought, sacrificing my mind to the void of this great empty space

A space that is in fact an abundance of wonder and life; worlds beyond imagination, a heaven full of grace

I've travelled far whilst walking this road of grief, covered a much greater distance than I ever thought

For somewhere along the route I've left behind the voice of despair and reached a lesson to be taught

I have learned that grief is a re-birth, a painful entrance into a new being, the stripping away of my old self

A lonely process that has broken yet healed, destroyed yet strengthened, tortured beyond anything else

And on this road that I am on, it is perhaps time now to turn around and return to where I ought to be

For I hear the cries of loved ones calling out to say `Time to let go, we miss you, please come back to me"

20th March 2021

LETTING GO

Like a postcard that is pinned to a noticeboard, I'm unable to move from under this pain of lead

So I lay helpless in my hour of suffering, with every goodness dissolving as I lay captured in my bed

Too early for the dawn I gaze upwards to the skies and beg for my rescuer to come and take me now

Is it God that I am pleading with, praying to, submitting my soul and heart to be freed somehow?

I am so tired, weary of hurt and loss that I need to muster all my strength to believe in a better time

Yet should I courageously cut the ties that bind and fly again some would see it as a cowardly crime

So I am trapped, snared by guilt of what harm I might do and I so hate this powerless feeling I hold

I am torn, confused for it is only a pathetic misplaced sense of love that stops me from acting so bold

But I am shrivelled up, a mere pathetic reduced form of the person that I once was and used to be

So how could it be so wrong to let me go and let me finally reclaim the power that I once held in me

Another hour has passed so I will close my eyes in the hope that sleep will come as my rescue

And I will say a silent prayer that perhaps, just perhaps I just might wake up, or not, as someone new

21st March 2021

THE SKYLARK

How beautiful is the Skylark for its message is the most uplifting of them all
For they sing their little hearts out, so excited to be alive, telling us to recall
How blessed we are that with each day, we can also sing so sweet and loud
We just need to open our hearts to nature and lift our spirits out of the cloud
This sweetest song full of zest for life matches their frantic wings that thrive
I am forever grateful for their message "Fly high, be thankful, enjoy being alive"

22nd March 2021

THE GRAVE – Poem written for Bob's Interment of Ashes

Remember, there is not one grave that ever holds life
It has no memories, or special times, or can be a beacon of light
It is but a reminder that time is short; to make every minute count
To feel grateful for life's blessings, even when there is doubt
Yes, it is a place where you can be still and explain away your fears
A sanctuary perhaps for your thoughts, prayers and falling of tears
But is it not where you will ever find me, although we are apart
For I am all around in everything; I am that whisper in your heart
I am in your laughter and smile when you mention my name
In that kindness you hold; the love you give despite the pain
I am in every sunrise and sunset; found with every dawn and dusk
For not a day will go by when I will not be in touch
For I am living inside you and it is there I can be found
Not in an earthly grave, or a sacred piece of ground
Remember, there is not one grave that ever holds life
It has no memories, or special times, or can be a beacon of light

1st May 2021

BLACKBIRD

I'm wondering if that blackbird knew I needed to hear their song; for the tune was bright and clear

Each note piercing through my army of grief, as if to declare war on it and fight away my fear

Oh little bird, I admire your bravery and faith that you could become such a warrior

But I fear I shall never sing again; my notes are dry, my voice weak, my words belong to a stranger

Yet still you remain steadfast in your cause; unphased; singing so beautifully in defiance

Outraged that I should be so dismissive, doubtful and dismayed by my lack of compliance

So surrendering I listen a little longer to your song; the song of life which heals my pain

And so today is a rare day; but a promising day, maybe, just maybe I might be able to sing again

2nd May 2021

CONFUSION

How I was fooled into thinking that I was doing ok, when I am nothing but a fragile mess it would seem

For the confident belief that I had stored in my head, was just a trick to the brain; a faraway dream

In a moment of lucidity, I can laugh at my thoughts, though the temptation to be free of this pain is so sweet

For this inner debate goes on and on fuelled by despair, until the heart finally breaks down in defeat

My grief is a tightrope that I walk one thousand feet up, sometimes I look down to see a way out

I sway, I quiver, and I barely know how, but I'm here, upright, moving forward in doubt

In doubt never knowing if I will ever reach the end, but my rope although narrow is secure

And this death cavern which I am crossing, needs to be defeated for everyone's sake I am sure

4th May 2021

THE CIRCLE

They say forgiveness is the antidote to anger, and love is the answer that can heal deep pain

But I'm caught up in a circle of torment, completely trapped, forever going round and round again

There's no forgiving, the hurt is too great, no inner love, self-healing; for all my strength has gone

Anger has manifested itself into pain, pain into hurt, hurt into despair and so it goes on and on

Despair into weakness and from there I am lost, for only a huge sense of self-loathing remains

Which in turn leads to anger and so the circle completes, and I am left here with my original pains

To break the circle isn't easy; there is no prayer of righteousness that my heart's ready to hear

But I hope that one day a certain prayer will come along; the one to make all my anger disappear

13th May 2021

I TALK WITH YOU A LOT

I talk with you a lot; we have conversations, discuss the way things ought to be
You wanting me to get stronger and happier, me needing somehow to be free

Free from the feeling of a crushed heart, a release from the torment of lost times
And so you come to me and offer help, in different ways and giving various signs

A robin will fly by, a white feather appears; a crazy comfort thought perhaps
But as days go by, I find solace in such things and feel guarded against a relapse

They say that acceptance is the final stage of grief, giving a new strength for moving on
And I find that against all odds, I am here still standing, still going forward and along

Along the road that I was destined to walk and I know you are so right when you say
"I am always with you, let me share the joys you discover, to live on in your heart each day"

14th May 2021

"Life is like surfing; you ride high on the waves most of the time but expect to come off the board now and then. The trick is to get back on it again"

– Bob Sheridan

17th May 2021

"Nature has just reminded me that no matter how fragile or small we may feel, we are still beautiful..."

17th May 2021

I love the resilience of grass; it bends rather than breaks, it gets cut down but continues to grow, it gets trodden on but still survives.

I think there may be a lesson here somewhere...

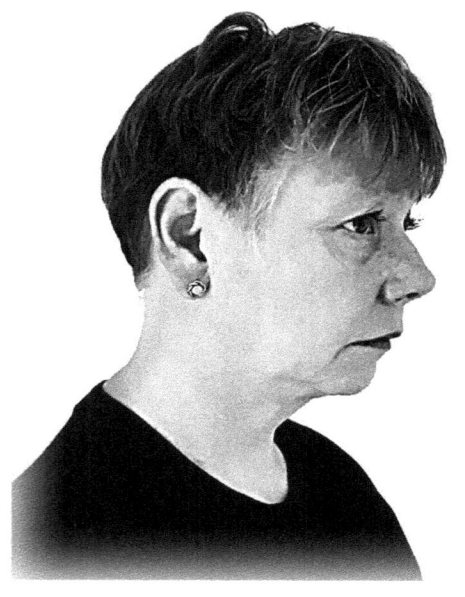
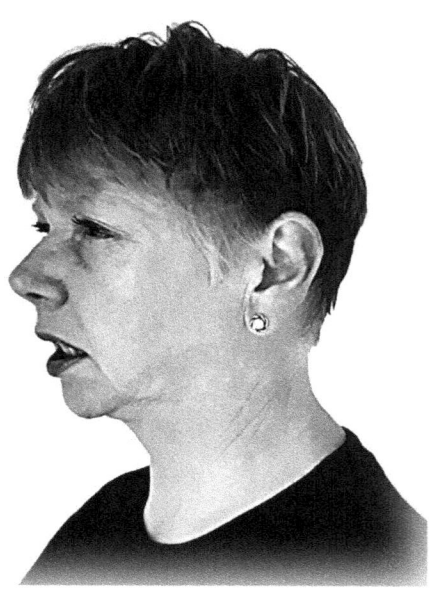

18th May 2021

THE STALKER

I confronted my stalker today, the invisible enemy within who constantly smirks when I begin to feel good

The self-loathing monster who glares back in the mirror saying "Really? Do you ever think you could?"

I realised that if I allowed myself to be followed by this constant fear of doubt, the dread of being a failure

Then I would be running for the rest of my life, a fugitive of my own mind, a persecutor against any endeavour

And so I began on a plan, a strategy to attack this tormenting barrier that kept me from ever feeling loved

I had to use the only power I had left, a brave step towards becoming a rescuer without being judged

And so the deep searching began, delving, excavating the ruins from a broken heart and years of doom

Not to find confidence, nor self-belief for those impostors had long since deserted me during my gloom

But to seek a new soldier to fight this battle of depression, to end the war that attacked my inner soul

And here amongst the debris of lost hopes, under the fountain of a million tears, I finally reached my goal

There lying in wait for my moment of trust, an exposed seed of love ready to be planted in a soil of faith

So I will now nurture this new found love, a love for myself, feed it, watch it grow and never let it escape

29th May 2021

SWEET DREAMS

Sweet dreams, nighty night; that was our final message at the end of the day
When everything was right with the world and all worries would fade away
In slumber I could release my dreams to the fantasy that lived beyond my mind
To a world where all the mental madness of life would softly be left behind

And then suddenly you were gone; your body said goodbye, leaving me each night to pray
That I will wake from this nightmare; have it disappear at the start of each new day

7th June 2021

YOUR HOUSE

Your house stands like an empty shell; soulless, for it belongs from another long, lost time

When the door was always unlocked and my breezy entrance always made you shine

Gone now are those vibrant bright days; those afternoons that would fill both our hearts

To brimming point with love and fun; beautiful times ripped away for now we are apart

I haven't managed to return since the day your home was stripped naked of all your treasures

The swift dissection exposing a lifetime of memories, a violation felt beyond any bearable measures

So now I gaze with sadness each time I pass by and try desperately to lift the heaviness in my heart

For you're no longer there, you are living with the Angels now and making a brand new start

But comfort can come in the strangest of ways, for in my mind's eye I still can recall those days

And from the power of the memory, I hear your voice "keep strong my darling, I love you" it seems to gently say

3rd July 2022 (how things change after a year)

And so it seems the hand of fate has held me gently whilst I struggled to keep a grasp onto living

And both your house and I have undergone changes from where we stood in the very beginning

No more emptiness, the old walls of pain gone; there's space now to walk and move forward at last

No more tears as I let your love carry me onwards, stepping bravely and away from the hurtful past

Love has once again returned within your house and laughter will be heard to echo as it should

It will vibrate with life as I am learning to do; I have rebuilt myself like I never thought I would

19th June 2021

SOMETIMES

Sometimes I feel I am running on empty, so depleted that I'm totally hollow inside

And every breath I take gets lost in this void, for I've struggled so much since you died

The weight of loss sits constant in my heart, although I hide my pain and sorrow so well

I will smile and say "Oh, I'm doing ok", for it is only your photo that I'm prepared to tell

To express just how hard I am coping without you and how my whole world has fallen apart

How incomplete I am without hearing your laughter, not having your smile to heal my heart

I know that by keeping you in my thoughts, I will also be keeping your memory alive

And I do realise that life must go on and how you would hate seeing me unable to thrive

So I am really trying to piece myself together, to be the woman you so loved and admired

That I am forcing myself to try and let go; let it be; fight on; despite feeling so very tired

For each day can be exhausting as I come to terms knowing that you're never coming back

And the nights can be so unforgiving; reminding me of just how much strength I really lack

22nd June 2021

CAN'T BEAR THE THOUGHT

I can't bear the thought that I'm never going to see you again, ever
It's a pain that sears through my heart,
Then travels though my body to claim it; destroy it, ruin it
Sever each vein of strength to tear it apart

I can't bear the thought that I'm never going to see you again, ever
That I must somehow cope without you
Never to share the dreams we had and repeat those treasured times,
But, live, survive with something anew

I can't bear the thought that I'm never going to see you again, ever
Are you in spirit somewhere near?
My world is unknown and so I beg you to come close to let me know
That yes, you are always here

I can't bear the thought that I'm never going to see you again, ever
That my heart breaks every day
I so need to know that we will be together on the other side once more,
That I cry, how I cry and constantly pray

I can't bear the thought that I'm never going to see you again, ever
So I let my imagination drift to let you in
And my heart responds and your image appears and once more you are near
Near enough to heal this wound within

22nd June 2021

THE FLOWER

I studied a beautiful flower this morning, really studied it. It was so intricate and a work of art

That I began to wonder about all the other wondrous flowers I see, yet never with my heart

The times I have glanced briefly and although their beauty cheered me for that given moment

I sadly gave no time to stop my thoughts or mission; I never allowed myself any involvement

And I think this is because I am confident that there will always be other occasions when I can rest

Further opportunities to put time aside to just stand and admire; and save that wonder for best

But how foolish I am; for the seasons of life are as delicate as each tiny petal and growing stem

For we each have a limited lifetime to blossom, to thank our God, our creator and whisper amen

Amen for the beauty, amen for the love; amen for the seed that creates life, no matter how brief

For life is short my friend; at times cut without warning, leaving behind the destruction of grief

And so let us teach ourselves to gaze in wonderment, never in haste, making only that quick glance

For nature deserves far more and our hearts need to thrive on its glory making a lifetime balance

29th June 2021

CONSTANTLY DANCING

I'm constantly dancing these days, sometimes through happiness, sometimes not
One step forward, two steps sidewards, some steps that I'd thought I'd forgot
Is it the dance of loss, one of reconciliation? Or one of learning yet again how to live?
I'm not sure any more and yet still I dance; releasing and giving all the best I can give

But I dance alone and that is the challenge that I am desperate to try and overcome
For without a partner to hold, I have only half the moves and flair that needs to be done
And yet I surrender myself to the music, the music of life that continuously plays
And will forever; and swirl around and dance for both of us until my closing day

5th July 2021

THERE WILL BE TIMES IN LIFE

There will be times in life when you must swim the sea of grief,
You will feel yourself drowning and going under.
But somehow you survive,
Somewhere you find the strength to keep on swimming.

Those of us who have ever been overwhelmed can see the land within our reach,
But we never know quite when we will get there….

5th July 2021

FRIENDS

Thank you to the friends who know about grief,
That it is a journey of ups and downs,
About treading carefully on an unknown path,
Sometimes the sad, sometimes the clown,

Sometimes never knowing who they have become,
But always aware that they have changed,
Working through questions of why and how,
Learning that no one can be blamed

Picking themselves up one minute, feeling strong
Next swept away by the tide of sadness
Smiling and laughing, feeling light once more,
Before crushed by the weight of badness

Yes, thank you to my friends who know about grief
That it's always messy and unpredictable
That it makes complete fools of the very best of us
It makes a kind heart irreplaceable

6th July 2021

THE LAST TIME

Last time I saw you I should have begged you not to die but to stay with me

Last time I saw you I should have held you so close and crushed you against my chest

Last time I saw you I should have told you how much I needed you to be with me

Last time you saw me you should really have tried to beat death and never have left

8th July 2021

LIFE GOES ON

On paper, I will survive this grief and the pain will ease, the loss will finally subside

On paper, the experts say, my heart will eventually heal from knowing that you died

In reality, my survival is slow, the pain is harsh and the loss beyond anyone's belief

In realty, my heart is broken into a million tiny pieces with no peace, hope or even relief

Have unconditional love some say, love yourself and your life will be full of light

Let the strength of your loved one carry you, help you through this hopeless plight

But right now, right this minute, it feels like a thousand razors have scored across my heart

And I am bleeding to death, inside, inwardly dying, unable to cope with being apart

I will try and sleep, for that is all I can do at the end of yet another exhausting day

Try and rest this heavy heart, let it bleed gently through the night until it is taken away

Away from the pain and into a slumber where dreams will often heal the hurt inside

As memories nestle close to soothe and wipe away every lonesome tear that's cried

11th July 2021

THE CLIFF FACE

The cliff face of grief is a place all of us visit in our lifetime
A time when we must grip on hard and climb and climb and climb
Picking our way carefully and strategically, fearful to look down
But losing our footing occasionally to plummet to the ground
But with every ounce of strength, we get up bruised to try again
For climbing is the only thing left to do, coping and living with pain
And the summit, distant and foreboding for much of the time
Will forever be the goal for many of us who have sadly been left behind

6th December 2021

THE BUTTERFLY

We all hold a butterfly within our hearts, a soft and gentle flutter
It dances amongst our inner thoughts to influence the words we utter
For love in its purest form is as gentle and as fragile as its wings
And just as wildly beautiful when allowed to spread and discover things

A spiritual magic surrounds the butterfly, as if they were from heaven sent
A gift from the Angels who have lent their wings with just one sole intent
To show us we will escape the dark and the struggle of crawling along
And by the pains of rebirth discover the place where our soul can safely belong

And so now I will gaze in wonder and smile whenever a butterfly is near
For I will feel you sending me the deepest love and know your spirit is here

BORROW YOUR RAINBOW (lyrics from original song)

In the desert of our minds, there are mountains we must climb
And all our hopes and all our dreams, can fall apart and rip the seams
Of our hearts
And with no place to go – I'll borrow your rainbow

When deep waters down below, come to drown the inner soul
That's the time to raise the game, take the dice and make your aim
To succeed… and have a go – and follow your rainbow

The calculator of time adds no reason or rhyme for the things we do
Any master plan is flawed if we try to close the door to something new

Little birds that take to flight, across the world with all their might
Hold more wonder in their wings, than all of our imaginings
Could try…And with no route to know – I'll borrow your rainbow

THIS LIFE IS NOT THE END (lyrics from original song)

I just want to talk to you, I want you to know,
I'm with you everywhere, every place you go
And if you ever wonder if we'll meet again,
I can say "for certain", This life is not the end
I can say "for certain", This life is not the end

I don't want to hinder you by calling every day,
But you know I stand beside you, when your thoughts come my way
The memories we've woven is a coat I wear today,
 And I wrap it close around you as your sleep empties the day
And I wrap it close around you as your sleep empties the day

Don't forget the sun may rise, the stars snuff out its rays,
But a timeless light for you will shine in my heart always
No matter where our journeys go and though I lead the way,
With a bond that can't be broken by your side I'll stay
With a bond that can't be broken, by your side I'll stay

March 2022

A PIECE OF MY HEART

I feel that I have now given grief its own special piece of my heart, its own little sanctuary where it can cry undisturbed. Where it can hold all the fear and disbelief that I sometimes feel. A place that can absorb all those moments that catch my breath and continue to cause hurt. A safe haven that allows the rest of my heart to keep on beating...and keep me living.

Acknowledgements and Thanks

I would like to give my immense thanks to some special people who have shown their love and support whilst writing this book.

To Gill McNab, Tom Johnson, Shane Mousley, Matt Hampson OBE, and Jackie Lymn Rose, for their beautiful friendship and support. To William Ivory for his unwavering encouragement in my writing projects, and to Brenda Cortez and Jean Sime for believing in me.

My gracious thanks to Dr Gillian Ennis for writing the Foreword and showing such kindness towards my work.

I owe so much to the talents of Kevin Becken; I am so blessed to have him as such a wonderful friend.

During my darkest days, Deborah Marsh was the light that made my path a little clearer and I call her an Earth Angel.

Finally, I need to give my heartfelt thanks to my wonderful husband who has been constantly by my side – his love, guidance and unfailing support are the most precious gifts I could ever have in life. Thank you, Andrew, for…everything.

ABOUT THE AUTHOR, TRACEY DENE POWELL

From the age of 14, I found that writing gave me an outlet for my emotions and so I have written songs and poetry for most of my life. I have been 'artist of the week' twice on BBC Radio Leicester, and my musical was performed in a national theatre in 2016. My song, 'Lead Me By a Rainbow', reached the semi-finals of the UK song writing competition, which was very special as it was written for my late sister.

In recent years, I have expanded my scriptwriting skills to enter into the world of comedy, and my plays have been performed in Rutland and Lincolnshire.

Over the years, grief has sent me along some very dangerous paths. When I was 27, I lost both my parents just three months apart. Then on 22nd May 2002 my sister lost her battle against cancer at the young age of 54.

2020 was a harsh year for everyone with Covid-19 entering into our lives like a bulldozer killing machine. For me, I had three deaths to face that year, and although not Covid related, the restrictions, isolation, and desperate fear that engulfed everywhere meant that saying "goodbye" to my loved ones was extremely hard. No hugs from friends and wearing masks sterilised every encounter made.

Contact Tracey:
www.traceydenepowell.com
tdp.music@btinternet.com